Dedicated To

My family, who has always supported me in all my endeavors and believed in me, even when I doubted myself.

To my friends, who have been with me through thick and thin, and have always encouraged me to pursue my passions.

And to all traders, who strive every day to become better and reach their financial goals, this book is for you. May it provide you with the knowledge and guidance you need to succeed in the world of technical analysis and trading.

HOW TO MASTER TECHNICAL ANALYSIS: A GUIDE FOR BEGINNERS AND EXPERIENCED TRADERS

UNLOCKING THE POWER OF TECHNICAL INDICATORS AND CHART PATTERNS TO ENHANCE YOUR TRADING PERFORMANCE

AVTAR KATARIA

Made with ♥ on the Notion Press Platform
www.notionpress.com

Contents

Preface

Technical analysis is an essential tool for traders and investors who seek to make informed decisions about buying and selling securities. As a SEBI registered Research Analyst with over 30 years of experience in the stock market, I have witnessed the power of technical analysis firsthand.

In this book, "How To Master Technical Analysis: A Guide for Beginners and Experienced Traders," I aim to provide a comprehensive guide that covers the fundamental concepts of technical analysis as well as advanced techniques. Whether you are a beginner or an experienced trader, this book will equip you with the necessary skills to analyze market trends, identify potential trade opportunities, and manage risk effectively.

From trend analysis to oscillators, from trading strategies to risk management, this book covers everything you need to know to become a proficient technical analyst.

I hope this book will serve as a valuable resource for traders and investors who seek to improve their understanding of technical analysis and gain a competitive edge in the market.

Acknowledgements

Writing this book has been a truly fulfilling experience, and I would like to take this opportunity to acknowledge the many people who have supported me along the way.

First and foremost, I would like to thank my family, particularly my daughter Natasha, who has been an invaluable partner in this project. Her insights and perspectives have greatly enriched the content of this book, and I am deeply grateful for her contributions.

I would also like to thank the OpenAI team for their tireless work in developing the advanced language model that has made this book possible. The cutting-edge technology behind this platform has allowed me to bring my knowledge and expertise to a wider audience, and I am truly grateful for the opportunity to share my passion for technical analysis with others.

Having been in the financial markets for over 30 years, I would like to acknowledge the many traders, investors, and market experts who have shared their wisdom and insights with me over the years. Your contributions have helped to shape my understanding of technical analysis, and have been a critical resource in the development of this book.

Finally, I would like to extend my heartfelt thanks to all of the readers who have picked up this book. Your interest and support are what drive me to continue to share my knowledge and passion for technical analysis.

Thank you all for your support, and I hope that this book will be a valuable resource for those seeking to gain a deeper understanding of technical analysis.

Sincerely,

Avtar Kataria and Natasha Kataria

Why This Book?

The field of technical analysis has been growing rapidly in recent years, and there is now an increasing interest among traders, investors, and market participants in understanding the principles and techniques behind this powerful investment tool. However, despite its popularity, many people are still unsure of what technical analysis is, and how it can be used to make informed investment decisions.

This book is designed to provide a comprehensive introduction to the world of technical analysis, and to help you gain a deep understanding of the key concepts, techniques, and strategies that are essential for success in this field. Whether you are a beginner or an experienced trader, this book offers a wealth of information that will help you to improve your trading skills and make more informed investment decisions.

This book covers a wide range of topics, including chart analysis, trends, technical indicators, chart patterns, oscillators and momentum indicators, candlestick charting, trading strategies, risk management, and the psychological aspects of trading. Each chapter provides a clear and concise overview of these topics, and includes real-world case studies and practical examples to help you apply the concepts to your own trading.

In addition, this book includes a comprehensive glossary of technical analysis terms, as well as a list of resources for further study, to help you continue your learning journey long after you have finished reading the book.

Whether you are looking to get started with technical analysis, or to take your trading skills to the next level, this book is an essential resource that will provide you with the knowledge and tools you need to succeed in the financial markets. So why wait? Start your journey towards a deeper understanding of technical analysis today!

CHAPTER ONE

Technical Analysis

1.1 Introduction

Welcome to the world of technical analysis, a discipline that has been used by traders and investors for decades to gain an edge in the stock market. Whether you are a beginner or have some experience with trading, this book is designed to provide a comprehensive introduction to the basics of technical analysis and its applications in the stock market.

This book aims to equip you with a thorough understanding of the fundamental concepts, tools, and techniques of technical analysis; so that you can effectively analyze stock market trends and make informed trading decisions. From chart analysis and trends to technical indicators and trading strategies, this book covers a wide range of topics to help you build a solid foundation in technical analysis.

Whether you are looking to invest in stocks for the first time or want to enhance your existing knowledge, this book provides you with the knowledge and skills to make informed trading decisions and maximize your returns. So, let's start our journey into the exciting world of technical analysis.

"The technical approach to the market represents the scientific method applied to the market." - John J. Murphy

1.2 Definition and History of Technical Analysis

Definition of Technical Analysis: Technical Analysis is a method of evaluating securities by analyzing statistics generated by market activity, such as past prices and volume. The primary goal of technical analysis is to use past market data to identify trends and make informed trading decisions. Technical analysts believe that market trends, as shown by charts and other technical indicators, tend to repeat themselves, and that by studying these patterns, they can gain insight into future market behavior.

History of Technical Analysis: The origin of technical analysis can be traced back to the late 19th century, when the Dow Theory was developed by Charles Dow, one of the co-founders of The Wall Street Journal. The theory suggests that market trends, both upward and downward, exist in the stock market, and that these trends are subject to recognizable and predictable patterns.

Over the years, technical analysis has evolved and expanded, with the development of new tools and techniques for analyzing market activity. The introduction of computer technology in the 20th century revolutionized technical analysis by making it easier to gather, process, and analyze large amounts of market data.

Today, technical analysis is widely used by traders, investors, and financial analysts around the world. While its use is not without controversy, many practitioners find it to be a valuable tool for making informed trading decisions, particularly in combination with other forms of market analysis such as fundamental analysis.

"The trend is your friend until the end, when it bends." - Ed Seykota

1.3 Overview of Technical Analysis

Technical analysis is a method of evaluating securities by analyzing statistics generated by market activity, such as past prices and volume. The goal of technical analysis is to use past market data to identify trends and make informed trading decisions.

Technical analysis differs from other forms of market analysis, such as fundamental analysis, which focuses on a company's financial and economic fundamentals. Instead, technical analysis focuses on price and volume data, and seeks to identify patterns and trends in the market that may be used to make trading decisions.

In technical analysis, charts are often used to visualize market activity and identify trends. Technical analysts use various tools and indicators to analyze chart data, including trend lines, moving averages, and oscillators.

While technical analysis has its roots in stock market analysis, it can be applied to a wide range of financial markets, including currencies, commodities, and bonds.

Despite its widespread use, technical analysis is not without its critics. Some argue that technical analysis is based on the idea that past performance predicts future performance, which is not always the case. However, many practitioners of technical analysis argue that it can be a valuable tool for traders and investors, particularly when used in combination with other forms of market analysis.

Overall, technical analysis is a field that requires a great deal of discipline, patience, and continuous learning, as market conditions and trends are constantly changing. But for those who are willing to put in the time and effort, technical analysis can be a powerful tool for improving trading and investment decisions.

1.4 Fundamentals of Technical Analysis

Fundamentals of Technical Analysis refer to the basic concepts and principles that underlie the practice of technical analysis. Some of the key fundamentals include:

Trend: Technical analysts believe that market trends, both upward and downward, tend to persist and that by identifying these trends, they can make informed trading decisions.

Support and Resistance: Technical analysts look for areas on the chart where the price has previously stopped rising or falling, known as support and resistance levels. These levels can be used to determine entry and exit points for trades.

Chart Patterns: Technical analysts study various chart patterns, such as head and shoulders, double tops and bottoms, and triangles, to identify potential trends and make trading decisions.

Indicators: Technical analysts use various mathematical indicators, such as moving averages, Bollinger Bands, and oscillators, to help them analyze market activity and make informed trading decisions.

Volume: Technical analysts also consider volume, or the number of shares traded, as an important aspect of market activity. High volume can indicate a significant increase in buying or selling pressure, which can be used to confirm trends or signal potential changes in market direction.

Price Action: Price action refers to the movement of a security's price, without considering any external factors such as news or economic data. Technical analysts believe that price action contains all the information necessary to make informed trading decisions.

Market Psychology: Technical analysts also consider the role of market psychology in the formation of trends and price movements. They believe that mass psychology, as reflected in market trends and prices, repeats itself and that this repetition can be used to make informed trading decisions.

By understanding these fundamentals of technical analysis, traders and investors can gain a deeper understanding of how to use this method to analyze market activity and make informed trading decisions.

1.5 Advantages and Limitations of Technical Analysis

Advantages of Technical Analysis:

Trends and Patterns: Technical analysis is based on the idea that market trends and patterns repeat themselves and by studying past market data, traders and investors can gain insights into future market behavior.

Objective Analysis: Technical analysis is an objective method of analyzing market activity, as it relies on past market data and objective mathematical indicators, rather than subjective opinions or emotions.

Widely Used: Technical analysis is widely used by traders, investors, and financial analysts around the world, and has a long history of success in the financial markets.

Time-Tested: The principles and techniques of technical analysis have been tested and refined over many years, and continue to evolve with the changing market conditions.

Complementary to Other Methods: Technical analysis can be used in conjunction with other forms of market analysis, such as fundamental analysis, to provide a more comprehensive view of the market.

1.6 Limitations of Technical Analysis:

Past Performance Does Not Guarantee Future Results: Technical analysis is based on the idea that past performance predicts future performance, which is not always the case. Market conditions can change quickly, and what worked in the past may not work in the future.

Limited Focus on Fundamentals: Technical analysis focuses on past market data, such as prices and volume, but does not consider the underlying financial or economic fundamentals of a security.

Can be Overly Complex: Technical analysis involves the use of many mathematical indicators and chart patterns, and some traders and investors may find it overwhelming or confusing.

Subjectivity: Although technical analysis is an objective method of analyzing market activity, the interpretation of chart patterns and indicators can be subjective and open to different interpretations.

Not a Standalone Tool: Technical analysis should not be used as a standalone tool for making investment decisions. It is important to consider other forms of market analysis, such as fundamental analysis, and to have a well-diversified portfolio.

Overall, technical analysis can be a valuable tool for traders and investors, but it is important to understand its limitations and to use it in conjunction with other forms of market analysis.

"Price action is the most pure form of technical analysis and the most reliable indicator of future market behavior." - Linda Raschke

1.7 Technical Analysis vs. Fundamental Analysis

Technical Analysis and Fundamental Analysis are two different approaches to analyzing the financial markets and making investment decisions.

Technical Analysis: Technical analysis is a method of analyzing market activity based on past price and volume data. Technical analysts believe that market trends and patterns repeat themselves, and by studying past market data, they can gain insights into future market behavior. Technical analysis involves the use of various chart patterns and mathematical indicators to analyze market activity and make informed trading decisions.

Fundamental Analysis: Fundamental analysis is a method of analyzing the financial health and performance of a company or security, based on its financial and economic data. Fundamental analysts focus on factors such as a company's earnings, revenue, debt, and economic indicators to make investment decisions. They believe that the underlying financial and economic fundamentals of a company will be reflected in its stock price.

1.8 Differences between Technical Analysis and Fundamental Analysis:

Focus: Technical analysis focuses on past price and volume data, while fundamental analysis focuses on a company's financial and economic data.

Timeframe: Technical analysis is often used for short-term and intermediate-term trading, while fundamental analysis is typically used for long-term investing.

Use of Indicators: Technical analysis uses mathematical indicators, such as moving averages and oscillators, to analyze market activity. Fundamental analysis does not use indicators, but instead relies on financial and economic data.

Objectivity: Technical analysis is an objective method of analyzing market activity, as it relies on past market data and objective mathematical indicators. Fundamental analysis can be subjective, as it relies on subjective interpretations of financial and economic data.

Complementary: Technical analysis and fundamental analysis can be used together to provide a more comprehensive view of the market. By considering both the past price and volume data and the underlying financial and economic fundamentals of a security, traders and investors can make more informed investment decisions.

In conclusion, both technical analysis and fundamental analysis have their strengths and limitations, and it is important for traders and investors to understand and use both methods in their market analysis and investment decisions.

Points to Remember

- Technical Analysis is a method of evaluating securities by analyzing statistics generated by market activity, such as past prices and volume.
- Technical Analysis has its roots in the stock market, dating back to the late 1700s and early 1800s.
- Technical Analysis can be useful in helping to identify trends, support and resistance levels, and potential buying and selling opportunities in the market.
- Technical Analysis is not a guarantee of future performance and should be used in conjunction with fundamental analysis and other forms of market research.
- Understanding key terms and terminology such as trend, support, resistance, and indicators is important

for using Technical Analysis effectively.

- Charting is an integral part of Technical Analysis, allowing traders to visually represent and analyze market data.
- There are several types of charts commonly used in Technical Analysis, including line charts, bar charts, and candlestick charts.

CHAPTER TWO

Chart Analysis and Trends

2.1 Introduction to Chart Analysis

Chart analysis is an important aspect of technical analysis that involves the study of market price data represented in the form of charts. This chapter aims to provide a comprehensive understanding of chart analysis and how to identify trends in stock market data.

Types of Charts: There are several types of charts used in technical analysis, including bar charts, line charts, and candlestick charts. Each type of chart has its own unique way of representing price data, and traders can choose the chart that best fits their individual needs and preferences.

Bar Charts: Bar charts are one of the most common types of charts used in technical analysis. They represent price data as horizontal bars, with the high and low prices of an asset represented by the top and bottom of each bar, respectively. The closing price of an asset is represented by a vertical line that is drawn inside the bar.

Line Charts: Line charts are another type of chart used in technical analysis. They are simpler than bar charts, and they only show the closing price of an asset over a given time period. Line charts are often used to show trends in stock prices over a longer period of time.

Candlestick Charts: Candlestick charts are a type of chart that is widely used in technical analysis. They represent price data in the form of candlesticks, with the body of the candlestick representing the difference between the opening and closing prices of an asset. The wick of the candlestick represents the high and low prices of an asset.

Chart Patterns: Chart patterns are recurring price formations that are created by the market's buying and selling activity. These patterns can be used to identify trends in stock prices and make predictions about future price movements. Some common chart patterns include head and shoulders, double tops and bottoms, and flag and pennant formations.

In this chapter, we will discuss the various types of charts used in technical analysis, including bar charts, line charts, and candlestick charts. We will also discuss chart patterns and how they can be used to make predictions about future price movements. With a strong understanding of chart analysis and trends, traders can make informed decisions about when to enter and exit trades in the stock market.

2.2 Types of Charts in Technical Analysis

Types of Charts in Technical Analysis are used to represent and analyze financial market data. Technical analysts use charts to identify patterns and make predictions about the future price movements of securities. In this chapter, we will cover the following types of charts:

Line charts: This type of chart displays the closing price of a security over a specified period of time. Line charts are simple and easy to interpret, but they do not provide a complete picture of price movements.

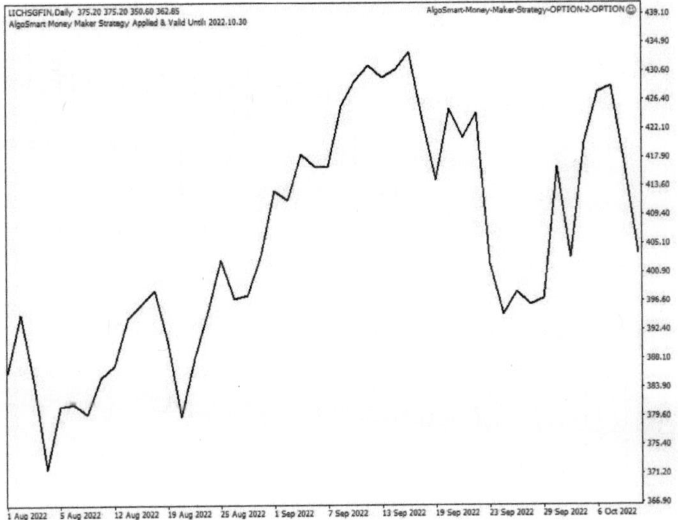

Line Chart

Bar charts: Bar charts show the opening, closing, high, and low prices for a security over a specified period of time. This type of chart provides more information than line charts, making it a popular choice among technical analysts.

Bar Chart

Candlestick charts: Candlestick charts display the same information as bar charts, but they use a series of candles to represent the price action. Candlestick patterns are a valuable tool for technical analysis and help traders identify potential buying and selling opportunities.

Candlestick Chart

Point and Figure charts: Point and Figure charts only show changes in price when a specific threshold has been met. This type of chart can help traders identify trends and potential breakouts.

Point and Figure Chart

Renko charts: Renko charts are similar to Point and Figure charts in that they only show price changes when a specific threshold has been met. Renko charts can be useful in identifying trends and support and resistance levels.

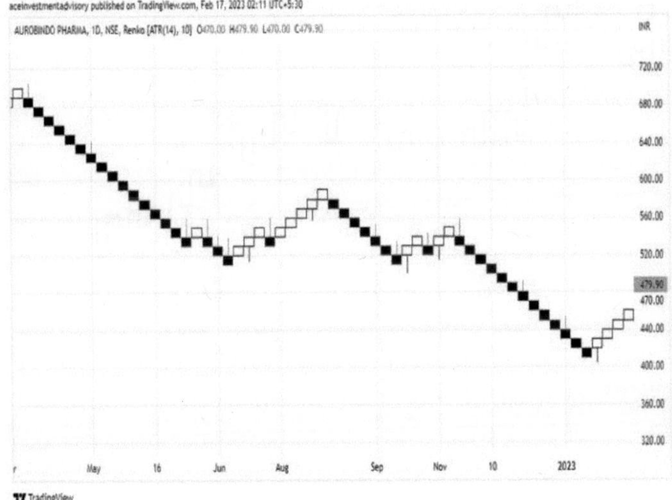

Renko Chart

Kagi charts: Kagi charts are similar to Renko charts in that they only show price changes when a specific threshold has been met. However, Kagi charts display the price action in the form of lines that change direction when a certain price level is reached.

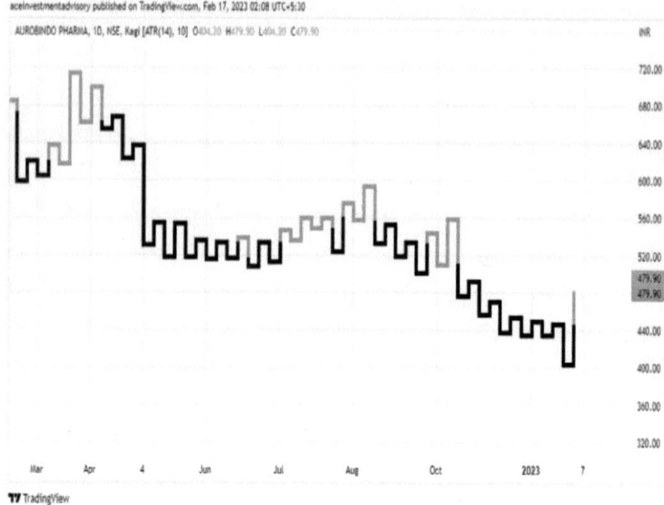

Kagi Chart

Each type of chart has its own unique advantages and disadvantages, and traders may choose to use multiple charts in their analysis. It is important to have a good understanding of each type of chart in order to make informed decisions when trading in the financial markets.

> **"Technical analysis is an art form that requires both knowledge and experience to be successful."**

2.3 Identifying Trends in the Market

Identifying trends in the market is a crucial part of technical analysis. A trend is the general direction in which the price of a security is moving over a specified period of time. Trends can be bullish, meaning that prices are increasing, or bearish, meaning that prices are decreasing. Understanding trends is important because they can help traders make informed decisions about buying and selling securities.

There are several ways to identify trends in the market, including the use of trend lines, moving averages, and momentum indicators. Trend lines are graphical representations of the price movement of a security over time. Moving averages, on the other hand, are mathematical calculations of the average price of a security over a specified period of time. Momentum indicators measure the speed and magnitude of price changes and help traders identify whether a trend is gaining or losing momentum.

Another way to identify trends in the market is to look at chart patterns. Chart patterns, such as head and shoulders, triangles, and flag patterns, can indicate whether a trend is likely to continue or reverse. Traders can also use candlestick charting to identify trends in the market. Candlestick charting is a type of chart that uses individual candles to represent the price movement of a security over a specified period of time.

In conclusion, identifying trends in the market is an important aspect of technical analysis. By understanding trends, traders can make informed decisions about buying and selling securities, and increase their chances of success in the stock market.

"Charts are the language of the markets, and understanding how to read them is essential for any trader."

2.4 Trend Analysis and Trend Lines

Trend Analysis and Trend Lines are fundamental concepts in technical analysis. Trend analysis is the process of identifying and analyzing the direction of the market trend, which can be either bullish (increasing prices) or bearish (decreasing prices). Trend lines are graphical representations of the trend that are drawn by connecting two or more price points.

The primary objective of trend analysis is to determine the overall direction of the market and to use this information to make informed trading decisions. This information can be used to identify potential entry and exit points in the market, as well as to determine the strength of the trend.

Trend lines can be drawn in various ways, such as by connecting the highs or lows of the price movement, or by connecting the closing prices. The most commonly used trend lines are support and resistance lines, which are used to identify potential turning points in the market.

When the market is in an uptrend, support lines are drawn to connect the lows of the price movement, while resistance lines are drawn to connect the highs of the price movement. When the market is in a downtrend, resistance lines are drawn to connect the highs of the price movement, while support lines are drawn to connect the lows of the price movement.

Trend analysis and trend lines are powerful tools in technical analysis as they provide valuable information about market conditions and help traders make informed decisions. However, it is important to remember that trend analysis is not a perfect science and that trends can change suddenly and without warning. As such, it is essential to use other technical indicators and analysis methods in conjunction with trend analysis to gain a more complete picture of the market.

"Price action is the most important indicator in technical analysis, and it reflects the sum total of all market participants' beliefs and expectations."

2.5 Moving Averages and their Significance

Moving Averages (MAs) are one of the most widely used technical indicators in stock market analysis. The purpose of using moving averages is to help smooth out the volatility of the price action and provide a clearer picture of the trend. MAs are plotted on a chart by taking the average of a set of price data points over a specified number of time periods. The moving average line is updated as new data becomes available and old data is removed from the calculation.

There are several types of moving averages, including simple moving averages (SMAs), exponential moving averages (EMAs), and weighted moving averages (WMAs). Each of these moving averages uses a different mathematical formula to calculate the average of the price data points.

The significance of moving averages lies in their ability to provide important trend information. For instance, a price crossing above its moving average can signal a potential bullish trend, while a price crossing below its moving average can signal a potential bearish trend. Moving averages can also be used to determine the strength of a trend and provide a visual representation of support and resistance levels.

In addition to trend analysis, moving averages can also be used as a tool for identifying potential buy and sell signals. For example, if the price of a stock is trading above its 200-day moving average, it may be a bullish signal for the stock, and vice versa.

In conclusion, moving averages play an important role in technical analysis and are widely used by traders and investors to identify trends, determine trend strength, and make buy and sell decisions. Understanding the different types of moving averages and how to use them effectively can be a valuable tool for anyone looking to improve their stock market analysis skills.

Points to Remember

- Technical analysis is the study of financial market data, including price and volume data.
- It uses various charting methods and statistical analysis to predict future market movements and identify trends.
- Technical analysts believe that market trends, as shown in price and volume data, can be used to forecast future market activity.
- Technical analysis can be applied to all financial markets, including stocks, bonds, commodities, and foreign exchange.

- The goal of technical analysis is to help traders make informed decisions about buying and selling securities.
- Some of the key tools and methods used in technical analysis include charting, trend lines, support and resistance levels, and moving averages.
- Technical analysis can be used in conjunction with fundamental analysis to form a complete picture of market conditions and inform trading decisions.
- It's important to remember that technical analysis is not an exact science and that past performance is not indicative of future results.

CHAPTER THREE

Technical Indicators

CHAPTER THREE

Technical Indicators

3.1 Overview of Technical Indicators

Technical indicators are mathematical calculations based on the price, volume, and/or open interest of a financial instrument. These calculations are then plotted on a chart, providing a visual representation of the data and helping traders to identify potential buy and sell signals. In this chapter, we will discuss the various types of technical indicators, their significance, and how they can be used in technical analysis.

Moving Averages

Moving Averages (MA) are one of the most widely used technical indicators. They are a type of trend-following indicator that plots the average price of a financial instrument over a specified time period. Moving Averages help traders to identify trends in the market and can also be used to generate buy and sell signals. There are different types of Moving Averages such as Simple Moving Average (SMA), Exponential Moving Average (EMA), and Weighted Moving Average (WMA).

Moving Average Convergence Divergence (MACD)

The Moving Average Convergence Divergence (MACD) is a trend-following momentum indicator that shows the relationship between two moving averages of a financial instrument's price. The MACD is calculated by subtracting the 26-period EMA from the 12-period EMA. A positive MACD indicates that the 12-period EMA is above the 26-period EMA, signaling a bullish trend. Conversely, a negative MACD signals a bearish trend. The MACD also has a histogram, which helps traders to visualize the difference between the two moving averages.

Bollinger Bands

Bollinger Bands are a type of volatility indicator that consists of a set of three lines plotted on a chart. The upper and lower bands are two standard deviations away from a Simple Moving Average of the financial instrument's price, while the middle line represents the Moving Average itself. Bollinger Bands help traders to identify potential buy and sell signals by indicating whether the price is trading near the upper or lower band. If the price is trading near the upper band, it may indicate an overbought condition, while a price near the lower band may indicate an oversold condition.

Relative Strength Index (RSI)

The Relative Strength Index (RSI) is a momentum indicator that compares the magnitude of a financial instrument's recent gains to the magnitude of its recent losses. The RSI is calculated by dividing the average gain over a specified period by the average loss over the same period. The RSI ranges between 0 and 100, with readings above 70 indicating an overbought condition and readings below 30 indicating an oversold condition. The RSI can be used to generate buy and sell signals and can also be used to confirm trends in the market.

> **"Technical analysis does not offer a guarantee of future performance, but it does provide a framework for making investment decisions based on historical data."**

Stochastic Oscillator

The Stochastic Oscillator is a momentum indicator that compares the closing price of a financial instrument to its price range over a specified time period. The Stochastic Oscillator ranges between 0 and 100, with readings above 80 indicating an overbought condition and readings below 20 indicating an oversold condition. The Stochastic Oscillator can be used to generate buy and sell signals and can also be used to confirm trends in the market.

These are some of the most widely used technical indicators in technical analysis. By understanding how each indicator works and its significance, traders can use them to make informed trading decisions and increase their chances of success in the stock market.

Moving Averages

Moving averages are one of the most widely used technical indicators in chart analysis. They are used to determine the average price of a stock or any other financial instrument over a specified period of time. Moving averages are calculated by adding up the closing prices for a specified number of periods and dividing by the number of periods.

The most common types of moving averages include simple moving averages (SMA) and exponential moving averages (EMA). A simple moving average is calculated by adding up the closing prices for a specified number of periods and dividing by the number of periods. An exponential moving average, on the other hand, gives more weight to recent price action, making it more responsive to price changes.

Moving averages are used by traders to identify trends, determine the strength of trends, and provide support and resistance levels. In an uptrend, the stock price will typically be above the moving average, and in a downtrend, the stock price will typically be below the moving average. The moving average can also be used to generate buy and sell signals. For example, a buy signal may occur when the stock price crosses above the moving average, and a sell signal may occur when the stock price crosses below the moving average.

In addition to trend identification, moving averages can also be used in combination with other technical indicators, such as oscillators and momentum indicators, to generate more accurate trading signals. By incorporating moving averages into their trading strategy, traders can improve their chances of making informed decisions and increase the chances of realizing profits.

Overall, moving averages are a versatile and powerful tool in technical analysis, and they are a valuable tool for traders looking to gain a deeper understanding of the financial markets and make more informed decisions.

3.2 Moving Average Convergence Divergence (MACD)

Moving Average Convergence Divergence (MACD) is a popular technical indicator used by traders and investors to analyze the trend and momentum of a financial instrument. It was first developed by Gerald Appel in the late 1970s and is considered one of the most reliable indicators in technical analysis.

The MACD indicator is based on the calculation of the difference between two moving averages of a stock's price. The first moving average (fast line) is typically calculated using a 12-day exponential moving average (EMA), while the second moving average (slow line) is calculated using a 26-day exponential moving average (EMA). The difference between these two moving averages is plotted as the MACD line.

Additionally, a signal line, which is a 9-day EMA of the MACD line, is also plotted on the chart. The MACD line is used to identify the trend, while the signal line is used to generate buy or sell signals. When the MACD line crosses above the signal line, it is considered a bullish signal and traders might look to buy the stock. Conversely, when the MACD line crosses below the signal line, it is considered a bearish signal and traders might look to sell the stock.

The MACD also includes histogram bars, which are used to visualize the difference between the MACD line and the signal line. The height of the bars represents the distance between the two lines and the direction of the bars indicates the direction of the trend. Rising bars indicate bullish momentum, while falling bars indicate bearish momentum.

One of the advantages of the MACD indicator is that it can be used to identify both bullish and bearish signals, making it a versatile tool for traders and investors. Additionally, the MACD is considered a reliable indicator, as it is based on moving averages and is not subject to whipsaws or false signals like some other indicators.

Despite its popularity and usefulness, it is important to note that the MACD is not a standalone indicator and should be used in conjunction with other technical indicators and analysis tools to confirm signals and minimize risk. Additionally, the MACD should not be relied upon exclusively and traders and investors should also consider fundamental analysis, market sentiment, and other market conditions when making investment decisions.

"Charts can provide valuable insights into market sentiment and identify potential trend reversals before they occur."

Bollinger Bands

Bollinger Bands is a popular technical indicator used in technical analysis to measure the volatility of an asset. Developed by John Bollinger in the early 1980s, Bollinger Bands are comprised of three lines: a simple moving average in the middle, with two standard deviation lines plotted above and below the moving average. These bands create a volatility envelope that adapts to market conditions.

The middle line, which is usually a 20-day simple moving average, serves as a baseline to measure price movements. The upper and lower bands are plotted as two standard deviations above and below the moving average, respectively. In a market that is trending up or down, the bands will generally widen, as price moves further from the mean. When price is moving sideways, the bands will generally tighten, as price oscillates within a smaller range.

One of the main purposes of Bollinger Bands is to help traders and investors determine whether prices are high or low on a relative basis. When prices move above the upper band, they are considered to be overbought, and when prices move below the lower band, they are considered to be oversold. Bollinger Bands can also be used to identify potential buy and sell signals. For example, a stock that is trading at the upper band and then moves back down to the middle line could be a potential sell signal, while a stock that is trading at the lower band and then moves back up to the middle line could be a potential buy signal.

In conclusion, Bollinger Bands are a useful tool for traders and investors looking to measure the volatility of an asset and to identify potential buy and sell signals. However, it is important to note that Bollinger Bands are just one of many indicators that should be used in conjunction with other technical analysis tools, as well as with fundamental analysis, in order to make informed investment decisions.

Relative Strength Index (RSI)

Relative Strength Index (RSI) is a popular momentum oscillator used in technical analysis to measure the strength of a stock or index. It was introduced by J. Welles Wilder in 1978 and is used by traders and investors to identify potential overbought or oversold conditions in the market. The RSI is calculated based on the average gains and losses of a security over a specified time period, typically 14 days, and is presented as a single line oscillating between 0 and 100.

A stock or index is considered overbought when its RSI is above 70, indicating that the price has risen too far too fast and may soon be due for a correction. Conversely, a stock or index is considered oversold when its RSI is below 30, indicating that the price has fallen too far too fast and may soon be due for a rebound. However, it's important to note that RSI alone is not a perfect indicator and should be used in conjunction with other technical analysis tools and chart patterns.

The RSI is also commonly used to identify bullish or bearish divergences. A bullish divergence occurs when the stock or index makes a lower low, but the RSI makes a higher low, suggesting that the downward momentum is losing strength and a potential reversal may be imminent. On the other hand, a bearish divergence occurs when the stock or index makes a higher high, but the RSI makes a lower high, suggesting that the upward momentum is losing strength and a potential reversal may be imminent.

In summary, the Relative Strength Index (RSI) is a useful tool for traders and investors to identify potential overbought or oversold conditions, and to spot potential reversals in the market. However, like any technical indicator, it should be used in conjunction with other analysis tools and chart patterns for a complete and accurate market analysis.

Stochastic Oscillator

The Stochastic Oscillator is a technical indicator that measures the market momentum. The indicator compares the closing price of a security to its price range over a set period of time, usually 14 periods. It is commonly used to determine potential overbought and oversold conditions in the market.

The Stochastic Oscillator is plotted as a line within a range of 0 to 100, with the overbought and oversold levels usually set at 80 and 20 respectively. If the Stochastic

Oscillator rises above 80, it suggests that the security is overbought, and a potential trend reversal could occur. Conversely, if the Stochastic Oscillator falls below 20, it suggests the security is oversold, and a potential trend reversal may occur.

One popular way to use the Stochastic Oscillator is to look for crossovers between the indicator line and its signal line, which is typically a moving average of the indicator. A bullish crossover, where the Stochastic Oscillator crosses above the signal line, indicates a potential buying opportunity. A bearish crossover, where the Stochastic Oscillator crosses below the signal line, indicates a potential selling opportunity.

It's important to note that the Stochastic Oscillator is not a standalone indicator and should be used in conjunction with other technical indicators and fundamental analysis to make informed trading decisions. Also, the Stochastic Oscillator can be subject to false signals and should be used with caution.

Overall, the Stochastic Oscillator is a widely used tool in technical analysis and can provide useful information to traders and investors regarding market momentum and potential trend reversals.

"The study of past price and volume data can be a valuable tool in predicting future market movements."

Points to Remember

- The three primary components of Technical Analysis: price, volume, and time.
- The purpose of Technical Analysis is to identify market trends and forecast future price movements based on historical data.
- Chart types and time frames: Line chart, Bar chart, Candlestick chart, and Intraday, Daily, Weekly, and Monthly charts.
- Trend lines and support and resistance levels: These are used to identify trend direction and potential price levels for buying and selling.
- Indicators: Moving Averages, Bollinger Bands, Stochastic Oscillator, RSI, MACD, and others, used to provide additional information about market trends and price movements.
- The importance of considering multiple indicators and time frames when making trading decisions.
- The significance of using proper risk management techniques in conjunction with Technical Analysis to minimize risk and maximize returns.

CHAPTER FOUR

Support and Resistance Levels

CHAPTER FOUR

Support and Resistance Levels

4.1 Introduction to Support and Resistance

Support and resistance levels are two important concepts in technical analysis that traders use to determine the price movement of a security. These levels are areas where the price of a security has a high chance of either reversing direction or continuing in the current trend.

Support levels refer to areas on a price chart where the price of a security has found a floor and has a tendency to bounce back up. This occurs when demand for a security is strong enough to prevent the price from falling further. The more times a security's price has hit a support level and bounced back up, the stronger that level of support is considered to be.

On the other hand, resistance levels refer to areas where the price of a security has found a ceiling and has a tendency to pull back. This occurs when there is a large supply of the security, causing the price to be pushed down. Like support levels, the more times a security's price has hit a resistance level and pulled back, the stronger that level of resistance is considered to be.

Traders use support and resistance levels to make decisions about buying or selling a security. If a security is trading near a strong support level, a trader may consider buying the security, as the price is likely to bounce back up. Conversely, if a security is trading near a strong resistance level, a trader may consider selling the security, as the price is likely to pull back.

It's important to note that support and resistance levels are not absolute, and the price of a security can break through these levels. When this occurs, traders must adjust their expectations and potentially change their positions.

In conclusion, support and resistance levels are important tools in technical analysis that traders use to make decisions about buying and selling securities. Understanding these concepts and how to identify them can greatly improve a trader's ability to make profitable trades.

4.2 Identifying Support and Resistance Levels

Support and resistance levels are key concepts in technical analysis and play a critical role in determining the direction of price movements in a financial market. A support level refers to a price point where buying pressure is strong enough to prevent the price of an asset from falling further. A resistance level refers to a price point where selling pressure is strong enough to prevent the price of an asset from rising further.

Identifying support and resistance levels involves analyzing past price data and chart patterns to determine where price has struggled to break through in the past. This information can provide traders with key price levels to watch for potential buying or selling opportunities.

One of the simplest ways to identify support and resistance levels is by using trendlines. A trendline is drawn connecting two or more price points and serves as a visual representation of the asset's price direction. When the price of an asset is approaching a trendline, it is likely to encounter either support or resistance.

Another method for identifying support and resistance levels is through the use of horizontal lines. Horizontal lines can be placed at the levels where price has made significant highs or lows in the past and serves as a visual representation of potential levels of support or resistance.

It is important to note that support and resistance levels are not absolute and can change over time as market conditions change. This means that traders must continuously monitor price action and adjust their support and resistance levels accordingly.

In conclusion, identifying support and resistance levels is a critical aspect of technical analysis that can help traders make informed decisions about buying and selling assets. By using trendlines and horizontal lines, traders can better understand potential levels of support and resistance and make more informed trades based on market trends and patterns.

4.3 Horizontal Support and Resistance Levels

Horizontal support and resistance levels refer to price levels where a stock has faced difficulty in moving past in the past. When a stock reaches a certain price level and fails to go higher, this level is referred to as a resistance level. Conversely, when a stock reaches a certain price level and fails to fall lower, this level is referred to as a support level.

These levels are significant in technical analysis as they can help traders predict future price movements. When a stock reaches a resistance level, it may have difficulty moving past that level and may instead fall back down. On the other hand, if a stock reaches a support level, it may bounce back up instead of falling lower.

Traders can use horizontal support and resistance levels to make informed trading decisions. For example, they may look to enter a long position when a stock reaches a support level or exit a long position when the stock reaches a resistance level.

It's important to note that support and resistance levels are not exact and can change over time as market conditions and sentiment change. As such, traders should be vigilant in monitoring these levels and adjusting their strategies as needed.

In conclusion, horizontal support and resistance levels play an important role in technical analysis as they can provide traders with insights into future price movements. Traders should be aware of these levels and use them to make informed trading decisions.

4.4 Diagonal Support and Resistance Levels

Diagonal Support and Resistance Levels refer to the lines connecting highs or lows in the price movement of a stock or an asset. This concept of support and resistance is not just limited to the horizontal level, but also extends to a diagonal pattern. The diagonal support and resistance levels are also known as Trend lines. The lines represent the level at which the price tends to face resistance or support and therefore, traders use it as a reference point to enter or exit the market.

To draw diagonal support and resistance levels, traders need to identify the trend in the market. If the trend is upward, the support line is drawn by connecting the lows, and if the trend is downward, the resistance line is drawn by connecting the highs. The lines can also be extended to predict future support and resistance levels.

Diagonal support and resistance levels are more accurate in identifying trend reversals and breakouts as compared to horizontal support and resistance levels. The slope of the lines indicates the strength of the trend and traders use this information to enter or exit the market. A steeper slope indicates a stronger trend, whereas a flat slope indicates a weak trend.

In conclusion, diagonal support and resistance levels play an important role in technical analysis and traders use it as a reference point to make investment decisions. Understanding the concept and the importance of diagonal support and resistance levels can help traders in making better investment decisions.

4.5 Dynamic Support and Resistance Levels

Dynamic Support and Resistance levels are key concepts in technical analysis and trading. These levels refer to areas where the price of an asset is likely to experience significant changes, either to rise or fall. This can be caused by various factors, such as changes in supply and demand, or the influence of market sentiment.

Dynamic Support and Resistance levels are different from Horizontal and Diagonal levels, as they are not fixed and instead change based on price movements. A dynamic support level is created when a downward trend in price is temporarily reversed, and a dynamic resistance level is created when an upward trend in price is temporarily reversed.

Dynamic Support and Resistance levels can be determined using various technical indicators and chart patterns. For example, traders may use moving averages, Bollinger Bands, or Fibonacci retracements to determine these levels.

When traders identify dynamic support and resistance levels, they can use them to enter or exit trades. For example, if the price of an asset is approaching a dynamic resistance level, traders may choose to sell the asset. On the other hand, if the price of an asset is approaching a dynamic support level, traders may choose to buy the asset.

Dynamic Support and Resistance levels are essential tools for traders to help manage risk and maximize returns. However, it is important to note that these levels are not always accurate and are subject to change, and traders should always use them in conjunction with other technical indicators and market analysis.

"Trends are your friend, and the earlier you identify them, the better your chances of making a profitable trade."

Points to Remember

- Understanding the types of charts and their uses: Line, Bar, Candlestick, and Renko charts
- Importance of identifying the market trend: up, down or sideways
- Understanding the key market indicators: Moving Averages, Bollinger Bands, and Relative Strength Index (RSI)
- Importance of support and resistance levels in determining market trends and making trading decisions
- Understanding trend lines and channels, and how to use them in technical analysis

- Understanding chart patterns, including flags, triangles, and head and shoulders
- The role of volume in technical analysis and how to interpret it in conjunction with price movements
- Understanding the concept of candlestick patterns and their significance in trading.

CHAPTER FIVE

Chart Patterns

CHAPTER FIVE

Chart Patterns

5.1 Introduction to Chart Patterns

Chart patterns are graphical representations of price and volume data that can provide a trader with important insights into market behavior and price movements. They can help traders identify potential trades, predict future price action, and determine appropriate risk and reward ratios.

There are several different types of chart patterns, including:

Reversal patterns: These patterns signal that a trend is about to reverse. Examples include head and shoulders, double tops and bottoms, and trend lines.

Continuation patterns: These patterns indicate that a trend is likely to continue. Examples include triangles, flag and pennant formations, and channels.

Complex patterns: These patterns are a combination of reversal and continuation patterns and can signal a change in trend direction or a continuation of a trend. Examples include multi-top and bottom formations, wedge patterns, and ascending and descending triangles.

To effectively use chart patterns in technical analysis, traders must have a strong understanding of price action and market behavior. It is important to understand the context in which a pattern is forming, including the underlying trend and market conditions, as well as to use other technical indicators and tools to confirm the validity of the pattern.

It is also important to be patient and wait for the pattern to fully form and for price to confirm the pattern by breaking out of the pattern formation. This helps to minimize the risk of false signals and potential losses.

Overall, chart patterns can provide traders with valuable information about market behavior and can be a useful tool in their technical analysis arsenal. However, it is important to approach chart pattern analysis with a disciplined and systematic approach, combining chart patterns with other technical indicators and tools for more accurate and effective market analysis.

> **"Charts are the language of the market, and technical analysis is the grammar and syntax by which we interpret that language."**

5.2 Head and Shoulders Pattern

The Head and Shoulders pattern is a popular and widely recognized chart pattern in technical analysis. It is a bearish reversal pattern that is used to predict a trend reversal in the stock market. This pattern is formed when the stock price makes three consecutive peaks, with the middle peak being the highest. The two lower peaks represent the shoulders, while the middle peak represents the head of the pattern.

The head and shoulders pattern is a reliable reversal pattern and is considered to be a strong bearish signal. Traders often look for the pattern to form over a period of several weeks or months, as it requires a significant move in the price of a stock or security to form.

To confirm a head and shoulders pattern, traders look for a downward trend in the price after the formation of the pattern. A neckline is drawn connecting the lows of the two shoulders. When the price breaks down below this neckline, it is considered a confirmed head and shoulders pattern, and traders will look to short the stock or security.

It is important to note that head and shoulders patterns can be found in both bull and bear markets, and traders should also be aware of false signals. To avoid false signals, traders should look for a volume increase during the formation of the pattern and a strong downward move in the price after the pattern is confirmed.

Overall, the head and shoulders pattern is a powerful tool for traders to use in technical analysis and can be a valuable tool in predicting trend reversals in the stock market.

5.3 Flag and Pennant Patterns

The Flag and Pennant Patterns are chart patterns in technical analysis that are used to identify potential price trend reversals or continuations. These patterns are formed by price movements that create a pattern resembling a flag or a pennant, hence their name.

A Flag Pattern is formed by two parallel trend lines that connect the highs and lows of price movements. The flag pattern is usually seen as a continuation pattern, indicating that the previous trend will continue after the flag pattern is completed.

A Pennant Pattern is similar to the flag pattern, but is more triangular in shape, with two converging trend lines connecting the highs and lows of price movements. The pennant pattern is also seen as a continuation pattern, indicating that the previous trend will continue after the pennant pattern is completed.

Both the flag and pennant patterns are useful for traders and investors to identify potential trend reversals or continuations, and can be used in conjunction with other technical indicators for confirmation. It's important to note that these patterns should be used in conjunction with other technical analysis techniques, and that they are not a guarantee of future market movements. Additionally, these patterns may not always form in perfect shapes, so it's important to use proper interpretation and discretion when using them.

5.4 Triangle Patterns

Triangle patterns are a commonly seen chart pattern in technical analysis that provide insight into the potential future price movements of a security. These patterns are formed when prices move between two converging trendlines, creating a triangle shape. The triangle pattern can be either symmetrical, ascending, or descending and can provide signals for both bullish and bearish price movements.

Symmetrical triangle patterns occur when the highs and lows of the security move towards each other, creating a triangle shape. This pattern signals a potential break in either direction, with the direction of the break usually determined by the overall trend in the market.

Ascending triangle patterns occur when the highs of the security remain constant, while the lows continuously increase. This pattern is considered bullish and signals that the security's price is likely to break higher.

Descending triangle patterns occur when the lows of the security remain constant, while the highs continuously decrease. This pattern is considered bearish and signals that the security's price is likely to break lower.

It is important to note that triangle patterns are considered continuation patterns, meaning they signal that the current trend is likely to continue. However, they can also signal a potential reversal if the trend breaks in the opposite direction.

In conclusion, triangle patterns provide useful information for traders and investors to make informed decisions. By carefully analyzing the shape and direction of the triangle pattern, traders can determine the potential future price movements of a security and make informed trades.

5.5 Double and Triple Top/Bottom Patterns

Double and Triple Top/Bottom patterns are reversal patterns that occur after an extended uptrend or downtrend in a stock's price. These patterns form when the price reaches a certain level multiple times, but fails to break through to a new high or low.

A Double Top pattern is formed when the price reaches a high level, retraces, and then reaches that same high level again before continuing its downward trend. The pattern is complete when the price breaks below the low point between the two highs.

A Triple Top pattern is similar, but with three failed attempts to reach a new high.

Double Bottom and Triple Bottom patterns are the reverse of the Double Top and Triple Top patterns, respectively. In these patterns, the price reaches a low level multiple times before eventually breaking above the resistance and starting an upward trend.

These patterns provide traders with a clear visual representation of price action and are used to predict trend reversals. However, it is important to keep in mind that these patterns can sometimes be subject to false signals, so traders must be cautious and consider other technical analysis tools to confirm their trades.

Points to Remember

- Technical analysis is a method of evaluating securities by analyzing statistics generated by market activity, such as past prices and volume.
- Trend is a persistent movement in a particular direction.
- The two types of trend are uptrend and downtrend.
- Support and resistance levels are key to identifying trends and potential trades.
- Moving averages are a commonly used tool to identify trends and track price changes.
- Trendlines are lines drawn on a chart that connect price highs or lows and are used to help identify and confirm trends.
- The concept of channel analysis involves drawing trendlines parallel to the primary trend to determine potential areas of support and resistance.
- Flag and Pennant patterns are brief pauses in price movement that can indicate potential trend continuation.
- The head and shoulders and inverted head and shoulders patterns are reversal patterns that signal a potential trend reversal.

- It is important to consider multiple time frames when analyzing trends, as short-term and long-term trends can provide different perspectives on market activity.

CHAPTER SIX

Oscillators and Momentum Indicators

6.1 Overview of Oscillators and Momentum Indicators

Oscillators and momentum indicators are technical analysis tools used to help traders and investors identify market trends, momentum and potential trend reversals. Unlike trend-following indicators such as moving averages, oscillators are designed to help traders spot overbought and oversold market conditions. Momentum indicators, on the other hand, measure the speed and magnitude of price changes.

One of the most commonly used oscillators is the Relative Strength Index (RSI). The RSI compares the magnitude of recent gains to recent losses, creating an oscillator that moves between 0 and 100. A reading above 70 is considered overbought, while a reading below 30 is considered oversold.

Another popular oscillator is the Stochastic Oscillator. The Stochastic Oscillator compares the closing price of an asset to its price range over a set period of time. It is designed to indicate whether a security is overbought or oversold by measuring whether the closing price is near the top or bottom of its price range.

The Moving Average Convergence Divergence (MACD) is another commonly used momentum indicator. The MACD measures the difference between two moving averages and is plotted against a signal line. The MACD generates buy and sell signals based on whether the MACD line crosses above or below the signal line.

There are many other oscillators and momentum indicators that are used in technical analysis, including the Williams %R, Bollinger Bands and the Commodity Channel Index (CCI). It is important to note that while these tools can be useful in helping traders and investors identify market trends and momentum, they should not be used in isolation. It is always recommended to use a combination of technical indicators and chart patterns to get a more comprehensive picture of the market.

> **"Charts are the language of the market." - Peter Brandt**

6.2 Moving Average Oscillator

Moving Average Oscillator, also known as the Moving Average of Oscillator, is a momentum indicator that helps traders and investors to measure the difference between a security's price and its moving average. This oscillator is created by subtracting a longer-term moving average from a shorter-term moving average. The difference is then plotted as a line that oscillates above and below zero.

The purpose of using a Moving Average Oscillator is to provide a visual representation of the momentum and trend of a security's price action. By using two different moving averages, traders can see the difference in momentum between the shorter-term and longer-term time frames. This difference can indicate whether the price is overbought or oversold, which can be used as a signal for potential trades.

Traders can use the Moving Average Oscillator in conjunction with other technical indicators to determine entry and exit points in the market. For example, a positive cross between the Moving Average Oscillator and the zero line is often used as a bullish signal, indicating that momentum is shifting to the upside. On the other hand, a negative cross between the oscillator and the zero line is often seen as a bearish signal, indicating that momentum is shifting to the downside.

Overall, the Moving Average Oscillator is a valuable tool for traders and investors to use in their technical analysis. By analyzing the difference between a security's price and its moving average, traders can gain a better understanding of the momentum and trend of the market.

6.3 Relative Strength Oscillator

Relative Strength Oscillator (RSO) is a technical indicator that measures the relative strength of a security compared to an index or benchmark. It is calculated by dividing the security's price by a weighted moving average of its price and then multiplying the result by 100.

The Relative Strength Oscillator provides traders with a measure of how strong or weak a security is relative to a benchmark, and helps to identify potential momentum and trend changes. The RSO oscillates between 0 and 100 and is plotted as a line chart. When the RSO is above 50, it indicates that the security is stronger than its benchmark, and when it is below 50, it indicates that the security is weaker than its benchmark.

Traders often use the RSO in combination with other technical indicators and chart patterns to make trading decisions. For example, a trader may look for a bullish divergence between the RSO and the security's price, where the RSO is making higher lows while the security's price is making lower lows. This could indicate that the security is strengthening and may soon reverse its downtrend.

Additionally, the RSO can be used as a momentum indicator, as a high reading indicates that a security is overbought, and a low reading indicates that it is oversold. Overbought conditions may signal a potential trend reversal to the downside, while oversold conditions may signal a potential trend reversal to the upside.

It's important to note that the RSO should not be used in isolation and that it is just one tool in a trader's arsenal. Other factors such as economic data releases, company fundamentals, and market sentiment should also be considered when making investment decisions.

6.4 Williams %R

The Williams %R (or the Williams Percent Range) is a popular momentum indicator that helps traders to identify potential overbought and oversold market conditions. Developed by Larry Williams, the Williams %R measures the difference between the closing price of an asset and the highest high of the last N periods, expressed as a percentage.

The Williams %R oscillates between 0 and -100 and is typically plotted as a single line on a chart. A value closer to 0 indicates that an asset is overbought, while a value closer to -100 indicates that it is oversold. In a bullish market, traders look for the Williams %R to rise from the oversold levels and cross above the overbought levels, as this may indicate that the trend is likely to continue.

The Williams %R is often used in conjunction with other technical indicators, such as moving averages or trend lines, to confirm market trends and support trade decisions. For example, traders may use the Williams %R to confirm a bullish trend when it rises from oversold levels and crosses above a 20-day moving average.

In conclusion, the Williams %R is a useful momentum indicator that helps traders to identify market conditions and potential trend reversals. By combining the Williams %R with other technical indicators and a solid trading plan, traders can increase the accuracy of their trades and potentially improve their overall results.

"The key to successful trading is to have a clear understanding of market trends and patterns."

6.5 Rate of Change (ROC)

The Rate of Change (ROC) is a momentum indicator that measures the percentage change between the current price and a past price. This is used to assess the strength or weakness of a stock's price trend. The ROC is calculated by subtracting the n-period price from the current price, and then dividing this difference by the n-period price. This results in a percentage that shows the rate at which the price has changed over the specified period.

The ROC is plotted as a line that oscillates above and below the zero line. A positive ROC indicates that the stock's price is increasing, while a negative ROC indicates that the stock's price is decreasing. The ROC can be used in combination with other indicators to determine the overall trend of the stock's price.

When the ROC is above the zero line, it indicates that the current price is higher than the price n periods ago. This is considered a bullish signal, and traders may interpret this as a sign to buy the stock. On the other hand, when the ROC is below the zero line, it indicates that the current price is lower than the price n periods ago. This is considered a bearish signal, and traders may interpret this as a sign to sell the stock.

It is important to note that the ROC can generate false signals in a ranging market, as the rate of change may fluctuate wildly without any real trend in the stock's price. Traders should also consider using other indicators and chart patterns to confirm signals generated by the ROC.

Points to Remember

- Oscillators are technical analysis tools that measure momentum, overbought/oversold conditions, and potential trend reversals.
- Some common oscillators include Relative Strength Index (RSI), Stochastic Oscillator, Moving Average Convergence Divergence (MACD), and Commodity Channel Index (CCI).
- Momentum indicators measure the rate of price change over a given period of time.
- Common momentum indicators include Rate of Change (ROC), Moving Average Convergence Divergence (MACD), and Relative Strength Index (RSI).
- Oscillators and momentum indicators can be used together to confirm signals and help traders make more informed decisions.
- When using oscillators and momentum indicators, it is important to avoid relying solely on one indicator and

to consider market context and other technical analysis tools.

- Traders should also pay attention to divergence between price and oscillator/momentum indicator readings, as this can be a sign of a potential trend reversal.
- As with all technical analysis tools, it is important to practice good risk management and use oscillators and momentum indicators as part of a comprehensive trading plan.

CHAPTER SEVEN

Candlestick Charting

7.1 Introduction to Candlestick Charting

Candlestick charting is a method of representing the price action of securities in a graphical format. It has become one of the most widely used tools in technical analysis, and has been used for centuries by Japanese rice traders. The candlestick chart is composed of individual candles, each of which represents a single day's worth of price data. These candles have a body and two shadows, which provide a wealth of information about the market sentiment during that time period.

The body of the candle represents the difference between the opening and closing price for that day, and the color of the body is determined by which of the two prices was higher. If the closing price was higher, the body is typically drawn as a hollow rectangle, or a "white" candle. If the opening price was higher, the body is drawn as a filled rectangle, or a "black" candle. The shadows of the candle represent the high and low prices for the day, and the length of the shadows provides insight into the volatility of the market.

Candlestick charts provide a quick and easy way to visually identify market trends and potential reversal points. One of the most popular uses of candlestick charts is to look for patterns, such as bullish and bearish reversal patterns, which provide traders with information about when it may be a good time to enter or exit a position.

In this chapter, we will examine the basic structure of candlestick charts and how to read them, as well as some of the most commonly used bullish and bearish reversal patterns. We will also discuss how to use candlestick charts in conjunction with other technical analysis tools, such as trend lines, support and resistance levels, and technical indicators, to gain a more comprehensive view of the market. Whether you are a beginner or an experienced trader, the information contained in this chapter will provide you with a solid foundation for using candlestick charts to make informed trading decisions.

> **"The art of technical analysis lies in recognizing repeating patterns and trends in the market."**

7.2 Bullish and Bearish Candlestick Patterns

Candlestick charting is a visual method of technical analysis that has been used by traders and investors for centuries. It is considered one of the most powerful chart patterns for identifying potential market trends and making investment decisions. In this chapter, we will explore the most common bullish and bearish candlestick patterns and how they can be used to gain a deeper understanding of market trends and make informed investment decisions.

7.2.1 Bullish Candlestick Patterns

Bullish candlestick patterns are signals of potential bullish market trends. These patterns are formed when prices rise over a specified period of time, such as a day or a week, and indicate that buyers are in control of the market. Some of the most common bullish candlestick patterns include:

Hammer: A hammer is a single candle pattern that signals a potential bottom reversal in a bearish market. It is formed when the price falls to a new low, but closes near the high, creating a long lower shadow and a small real body.

Hammer

Bullish Engulfing: The bullish engulfing pattern is formed by two candles, with the second candle completely covering the real body of the first candle. This pattern indicates a potential change in trend from bearish to bullish.

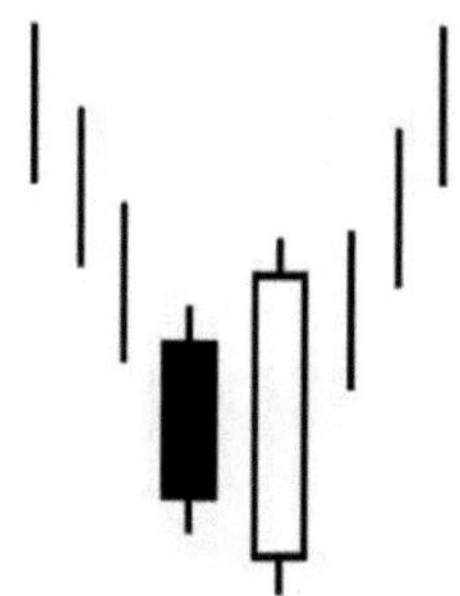

Bullish Engulfing

Morning Star: The morning star pattern is a three-candle formation that signals a potential bottom reversal in a bearish market. It is formed by a small real body candle, followed by a large real body candle, and finally a small real body candle that closes near the high.

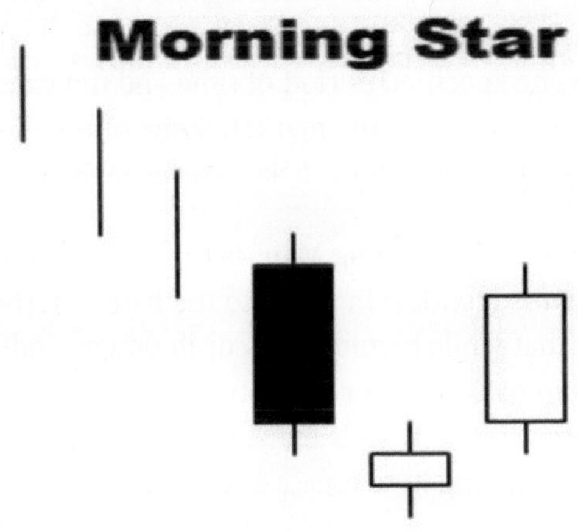

Morning Star

7.2.2 Bearish Candlestick Patterns

Bearish candlestick patterns are signals of potential bearish market trends. These patterns are formed when prices fall over a specified period of time and indicate that sellers are in control of the market. Some of the most common bearish candlestick patterns include:

Hanging Man: The "Hanging Man" is the name given to a candle that is identical in shape to the hammer, the difference is that while hammers occur in downtrends, the Hanging Man pattern occurs in uptrends. It is often the first sign that the uptrend is exhausting, and bears are stepping in to create a reversal.

For the reversal signal to be confirmed, the consequent bearish bar should reach the "neckline" established by the open of the bullish bar on the other side of the hanging man.

Hanging Man

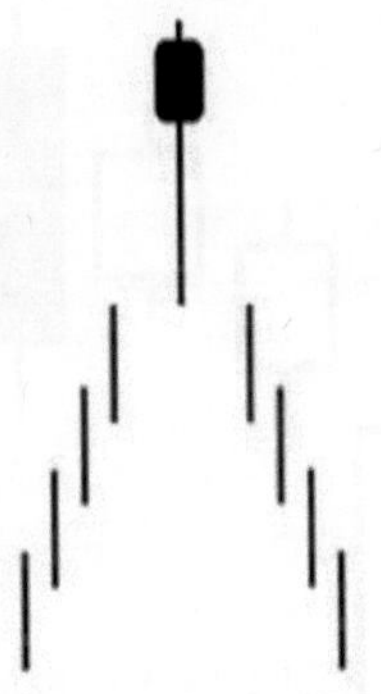

Hanging Man

Bearish Engulfing: The bearish engulfing pattern is formed by two candles, with the second candle completely covering the real body of the first candle. This pattern indicates a potential change in trend from bullish to bearish.

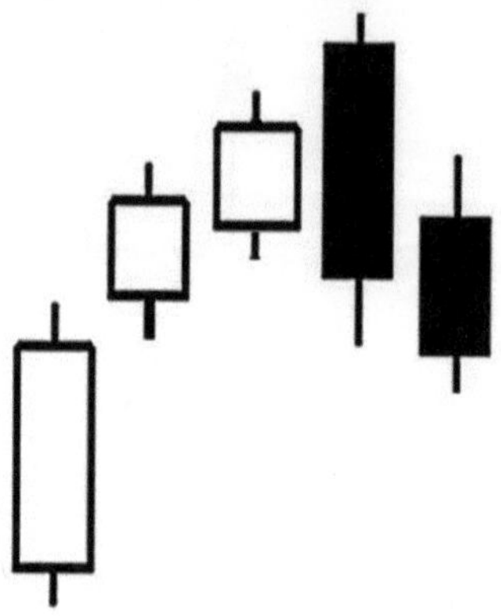

Bearish Engulfing

Evening Star: The evening star pattern is a three-candle formation that signals a potential top reversal in a bullish market. It is formed by a small real body candle, followed by a large real body candle, and finally a small real body candle that closes near the low.

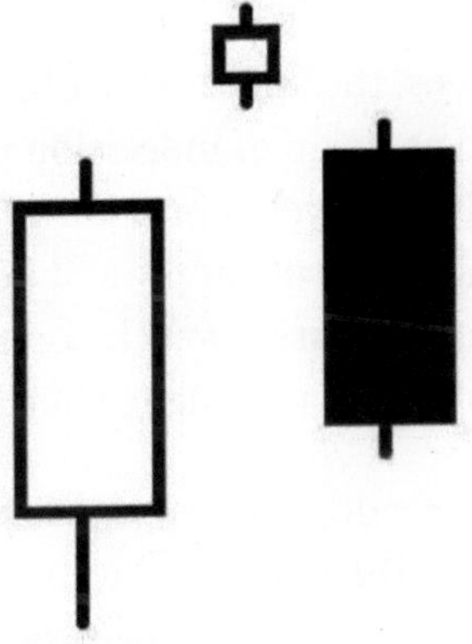

Evening Star

It is important to note that candlestick patterns are best used in conjunction with other technical analysis tools and techniques. They are not a guarantee of market trends, but rather a visual representation of market sentiment and supply and demand dynamics.

7.3 Doji Candlestick Pattern

Doji is a Japanese word for "at the same time," and it refers to a type of candlestick pattern that is commonly used in technical analysis. A doji pattern is formed when the opening price and closing price of a stock or other financial instrument are exactly the same, or very close to each other. This creates a candle-like shape that is usually accompanied by long upper and lower shadows.

In technical analysis, the appearance of a doji pattern is often interpreted as a sign of indecision in the market, indicating that neither buyers nor sellers are in control. It suggests that the forces of supply and demand are in balance, and that the market may be on the verge of a reversal or a major change in trend.

The interpretation of a doji pattern can vary depending on the overall context of the market, as well as the position of the doji in relation to other price patterns and technical indicators. For example, a doji that appears after a long uptrend may indicate a potential top or reversal, while a doji that appears during a downtrend may suggest a possible bottom or reversal.

In addition to the standard doji pattern, there are several variations, such as the dragonfly doji and the gravestone doji, each of which may have slightly different implications for the market. It is important to use multiple technical indicators and tools when interpreting doji patterns, as well as to understand the overall context of the market and the stock or financial instrument being analyzed.

Structure and Types

A doji candle is dominated by wicks with very small bodies or no bodies at all. This formation can occur at the end of a downtrend, as well in the closing stages of the uptrend.

Neutral Doji

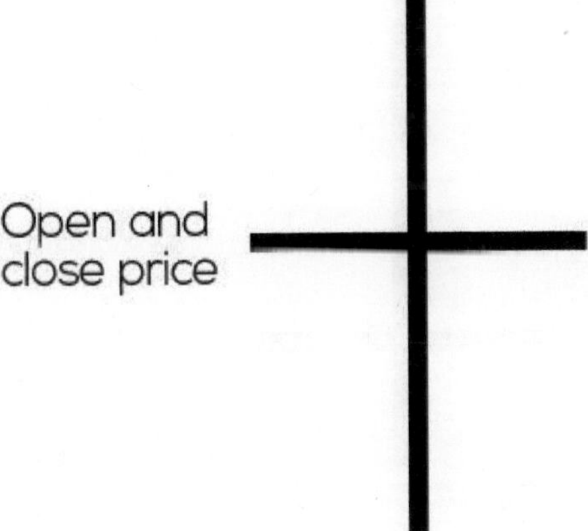

Neutral Doji

Gravestone Doji

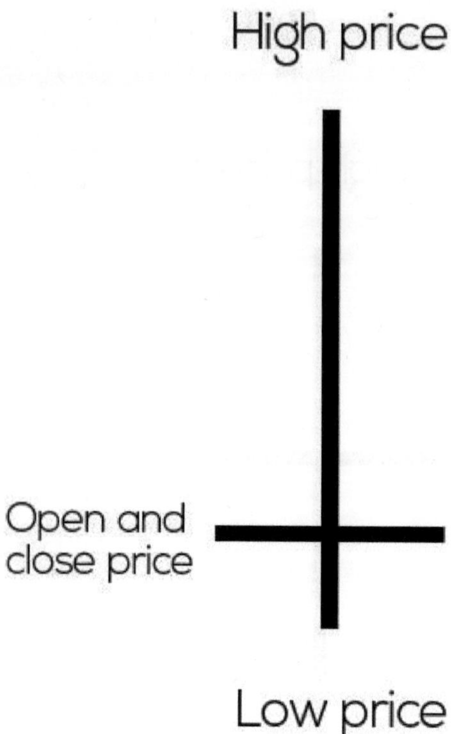

Gravestone Doji

Long-Legged Doji

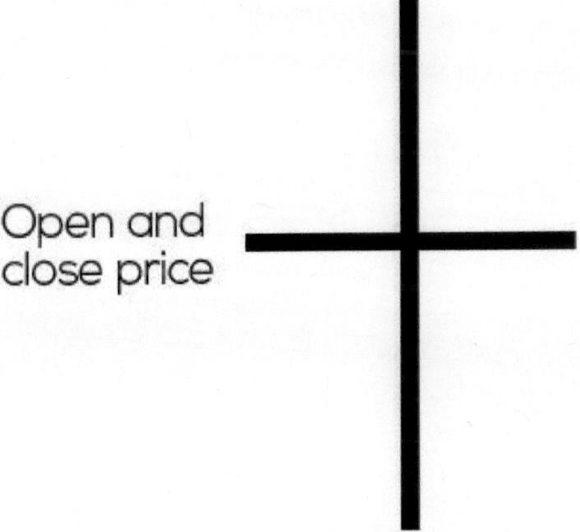

Long-Legged Doji

Dragonfly Doji

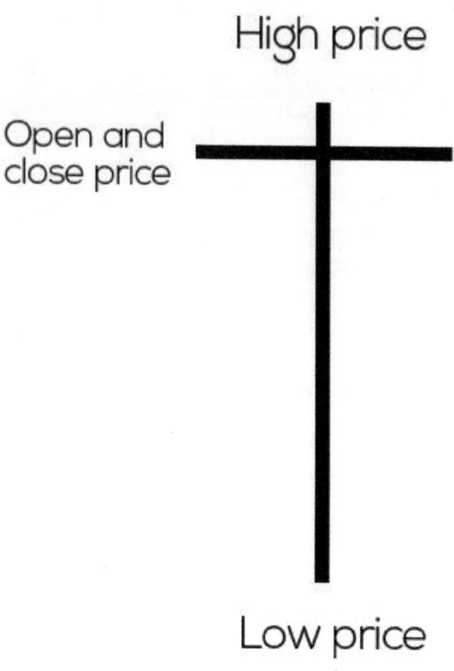

Dragonfly Doji

Candlestick charting is a popular method of technical analysis used by traders and investors to gain insight into market trends and potential price movements. One important aspect of candlestick charting is the identification of bullish and bearish candlestick patterns.

Bullish candlestick patterns, such as the Bullish Engulfing and Hammer patterns, indicate that the market is moving in an upward direction and that prices are likely to continue to rise. The Bullish Engulfing pattern consists of a small red candlestick followed by a larger green candlestick, with the green candlestick completely engulfing the red one. The Hammer pattern is identified by a small body, long lower shadow, and no upper shadow, indicating that the market has bottomed out and prices are likely to rise.

Bearish candlestick patterns, such as the Bearish Engulfing and Hanging Man patterns, indicate that the market is moving in a downward direction and that prices are likely to continue to fall. The Bearish Engulfing pattern consists of a small green candlestick followed by a larger red candlestick, with the red candlestick completely engulfing the green one. The Hanging Man pattern is identified by a small body, long upper shadow, and no lower shadow, indicating that the market has topped out and prices are likely to fall.

Another important candlestick pattern is the Doji pattern. The Doji pattern is formed when the opening and closing prices are the same or nearly the same, creating a cross or plus sign on the chart. This pattern indicates a reversal in market trend and a potential change in direction.

In conclusion, the identification of bullish and bearish candlestick patterns, as well as the Doji pattern, can provide valuable information to traders and investors in their decision-making process. By understanding the signals and implications of these patterns, traders can make informed decisions and potentially profit from market movements.

7.4 Marubozu Candlestick Pattern

Marubozu Candlestick Pattern is a single-bodied candlestick pattern that represents a strong bullish or bearish trend in the market. It is formed when the high and low prices of a security are very close to each other and the opening and closing prices are at either the high or low end of the price range.

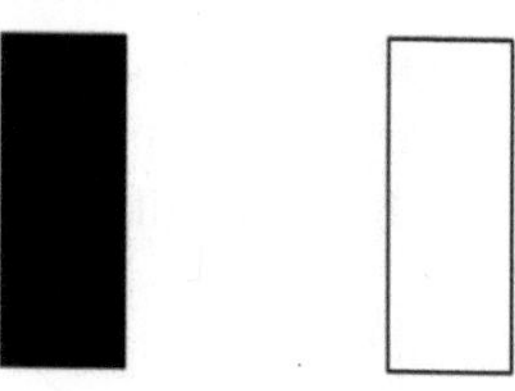

Marubozu Candle

The name Marubozu, which means "shaved head" in Japanese, refers to the fact that the wicks or shadows on the top and bottom of the candlestick are very small or non-existent. This indicates that the price has been traded actively and steadily in a single direction for the entire trading period, either up or down.

Bullish Marubozu is formed when the opening price is at the low end of the price range and the closing price is at the high end, creating a long white body. This indicates that the buyers dominated the market throughout the trading period and pushed the price up.

On the other hand, Bearish Marubozu is formed when the opening price is at the high end of the price range and the closing price is at the low end, creating a long black body. This indicates that the sellers dominated the market throughout the trading period and pushed the price down.

The Marubozu pattern is considered to be a strong bullish or bearish signal and is often used by traders to confirm the existing trend or to initiate a new position. However, it is important to note that like all technical analysis tools, Marubozu Candlestick Pattern should not be used in isolation and should be used in conjunction with other technical indicators and analysis methods to make informed trading decisions.

> "Patience and discipline are crucial qualities for any trader who wants to succeed in the long run."

Points to Remember

- Candlestick charts are an important tool in technical analysis that provide information on price and market sentiment.
- Japanese candlestick patterns, such as the Bullish Engulfing and Bearish Engulfing patterns, provide valuable insights into the direction of market trends.
- Doji candlestick patterns are considered to be important indicators of market indecision and potential trend reversals.
- Hammer and Hanging Man patterns can be used to identify support and resistance levels and potential trend changes.
- The Marubozu pattern is a strong indicator of market momentum in a single direction.
- Traders should consider multiple candlestick patterns in combination with other technical analysis tools and market indicators to form a comprehensive view of the

market.

- It is important to understand the context of the market and to avoid making decisions based solely on a single pattern or indicator.

CHAPTER EIGHT

Trading Strategies Using Technical Analysis

8.1 Introduction to Trading Strategies

Trading strategies are the backbone of any successful trader, and technical analysis provides a wealth of information to help traders make informed decisions. In this chapter, we will look at how traders can use the knowledge gained from technical analysis to build effective trading strategies.

One common approach is to combine chart analysis and technical indicators to identify entry and exit points in the market. For example, a trader may look for a bullish trend in the market, indicated by a rising trend line on the chart, and then use technical indicators like the Relative Strength Index (RSI) or Moving Average Convergence Divergence (MACD) to confirm the trend and identify potential entry points.

Another popular strategy is to trade chart patterns, like head and shoulders or flag and pennant patterns, which can signal a potential trend reversal. Traders can use technical indicators to confirm the pattern and make a trade based on the expected market move.

Oscillators and momentum indicators can also be used to build effective trading strategies. For example, a trader may look for a stock that is overbought, as indicated by a high reading on the Relative Strength Oscillator, and then sell the stock when the RSI falls back into a more normal range. Similarly, a trader may look for a stock that is oversold, as indicated by a low reading on the Williams %R indicator, and then buy the stock when the Williams %R rises back into a more normal range.

It is important to note that no single trading strategy works in all market conditions. Traders should be flexible and willing to adjust their strategies based on market conditions and changes in the underlying securities. Additionally, it is important to have a solid understanding of risk management techniques to protect against potential losses.

In conclusion, technical analysis provides a wealth of information for traders looking to build effective trading strategies. Whether you choose to trade chart patterns, use technical indicators, or combine the two, the key to success is to have a solid understanding of the tools and techniques available, and the ability to adapt to changing market conditions.

8.2 Trend Following Strategy

A Trend Following Strategy is a popular method of trading stocks and other securities that uses technical analysis to identify the direction of the market. The strategy assumes that market trends tend to persist over time and can be used to predict future market movements.

The basic idea of this strategy is to buy securities when they are trending upwards and to sell them when they are trending downwards. This can be achieved by using trend lines, moving averages and other technical indicators to identify the direction of the trend.

Once the trend has been identified, traders can use stop-loss orders to limit their risk and set their profit target to lock in gains. This strategy can be applied to a range of different time frames, including daily, weekly, and monthly charts.

One of the benefits of this strategy is that it is relatively simple and straightforward, and can be applied by both novice and experienced traders. However, it is important to keep in mind that no single strategy is foolproof, and all trading strategies come with a certain degree of risk.

Overall, a Trend Following Strategy can be a useful tool for traders looking to capitalize on market trends and generate profits from their investments. However, it is important to approach trading with caution, and to always take a disciplined and well-informed approach to managing risk and maximizing returns.

8.3 Breakout Strategy

The Breakout Strategy is a popular trading technique used by traders to identify and capitalize on significant market moves. It is based on the idea that when the price of a security breaks above or below a key level, such as a resistance or support level, it signals a potential trend change.

The Breakout Strategy is implemented by first identifying the key levels of support and resistance for the security being traded. The trader then waits for the price to break out of these levels, either to the upside or downside. Once the price has broken out, the trader buys (if the price broke out to the upside) or sells (if the price broke out to the downside) the security.

The key to a successful Breakout Strategy is to identify the key levels accurately, as well as determining the right moment to enter the trade. Traders should look for high volume and strong momentum to confirm the breakout, as this can reduce the likelihood of false breakouts.

In addition, traders should also have a well-defined risk management plan, including stop-loss orders, to mitigate potential losses in case the breakout turns out to be false. Overall, the Breakout Strategy can be a useful tool for traders who are looking to capitalize on significant market moves and generate profits in the stock market.

"The market is always right." - Richard Wyckoff

8.4 Mean Reversion Strategy

Mean reversion is a popular trading strategy used by technical analysts and traders to identify and take advantage of potential profit opportunities in the stock market. The basic premise of the mean reversion strategy is that the stock market tends to revert back to its average price or mean over time. The theory behind this is that the stock market, like all other financial markets, is subject to the laws of supply and demand. When the price of a stock is well above its average, there is an increased supply, and when the price is well below its average, there is an increased demand.

The mean reversion strategy works by identifying when a stock's price is significantly above or below its average and then entering a position in the opposite direction. This can be done through the use of technical indicators such as moving averages or Bollinger Bands.

Traders who use the mean reversion strategy will often wait for the price of a stock to reach its extreme level and then enter a trade in the opposite direction. For example, if the stock is trading well above its average, a trader may enter a short position in anticipation of a price correction back to its average. On the other hand, if the stock is trading well below its average, a trader may enter a long position in anticipation of a price move back to its average.

Mean reversion can be a useful trading strategy for traders who are looking for a more systematic approach to the stock market. However, like all trading strategies, it is important to understand the risks involved and to have a well-defined plan for risk management. Additionally, it is important to keep in mind that mean reversion is not a guarantee of success and that there are times when the market will not revert back to its average price.

8.5 Moving Average Crossover Strategy

The Moving Average Crossover strategy is a popular technical analysis trading strategy that is used by many traders to identify potential buying or selling opportunities in the market. The strategy is based on the idea that the stock price will tend to follow a trend and that trends can be detected using moving averages. The strategy uses two moving averages, a short-term moving average and a long-term moving average, to determine the trend of the stock price. If the short-term moving average crosses above the long-term moving average, it is considered a bullish signal and traders might consider buying the stock. On the other hand, if the short-term moving average crosses below the long-term moving average, it is considered a bearish signal and traders might consider selling the stock.

One of the advantages of the Moving Average Crossover strategy is that it is a simple and straightforward way of identifying trends in the market. It is also widely used by traders because it can help to filter out noise and provide a clearer picture of the market trend. Additionally, this strategy can be used in different types of markets, whether the market is trending up or down.

However, it is important to note that the Moving Average Crossover strategy should not be relied upon as the sole source of information for making trading decisions. Traders should also consider other technical indicators, chart patterns, and fundamental analysis before making a trade. Additionally, traders should also keep in mind that moving averages are lagging indicators and may not provide the most up-to-date information about the market trend.

Points to Remember

- Technical analysis is a tool used to analyze market data and forecast future price movements. There are various strategies traders can use to take advantage of this information.
- Trend following strategies involve identifying trends in the market and trading in the direction of the trend. Moving averages and trend lines are common tools used to identify trends.
- Mean reversion strategies involve identifying situations where the price has moved too far from its average, and assuming that it will return to its mean. Bollinger Bands and the Relative Strength Index (RSI) are commonly used to identify mean reversion opportunities.
- Breakout strategies involve identifying key support and resistance levels, and entering trades when the price breaks through these levels. This can be a profitable strategy when markets are volatile.
- Moving Average Crossover strategies involve using two or more moving averages to identify changes in trend. Traders can use this strategy to take advantage of trends in the market and avoid entering trades during choppy periods.
- It's important to remember that no trading strategy is foolproof, and that market conditions can change

quickly. Traders should always use risk management techniques and be prepared to adjust their strategies as needed.

- Backtesting and forward testing are important tools to evaluate the effectiveness of trading strategies. Traders can use these tools to see how a strategy would have performed in the past, and to assess its potential for the future.
- Ultimately, the key to success in trading is having a solid understanding of technical analysis and a disciplined approach to trading. By using a combination of technical indicators and trading strategies, traders can improve their chances of success in the market.

CHAPTER NINE

Risk Management and Psychological Aspects of Trading

9.1 Introduction to Risk Management

In the stock market, technical analysis is just one aspect of successful trading. Equally important is the management of risk and the psychological preparation required to be a successful trader. This chapter will explore the key concepts of risk management and the psychology of trading.

Risk Management: Risk management is a crucial aspect of trading in the stock market. It involves identifying, assessing and prioritizing potential risks, and then taking appropriate action to minimize or mitigate those risks. There are various methods of risk management, including position sizing, stop-loss orders and diversification.

Position Sizing: Position sizing is the process of determining the appropriate size of a trade in relation to the size of your overall portfolio. This helps to minimize the impact of any individual trade on your overall portfolio, and reduces the risk of a large loss.

Stop-Loss Orders: Stop-loss orders are a type of order that automatically closes a trade when a specific price is reached. This helps to minimize potential losses by automatically closing a trade when it reaches a certain point.

Diversification: Diversification is the process of spreading your investments across a range of different stocks, bonds and other financial instruments. This helps to reduce the risk of loss by spreading your investments across a range of assets, rather than having all your eggs in one basket.

Psychology of Trading: Trading in the stock market can be a challenging and emotionally charged experience, and it is important to understand and manage the psychological aspects of trading. Some of the key psychological challenges that traders face include fear, greed, and overconfidence.

Fear: Fear is a common psychological challenge in trading. Fear of loss can lead traders to make poor decisions, such as selling too early or holding onto losing positions for too long.

Greed: Greed can also be a problem in trading. Greed can lead traders to take on too much risk, ignore their risk management strategies, and make impulsive decisions based on emotions rather than sound analysis.

Overconfidence: Overconfidence is a common psychological challenge for traders, especially for those who have had success in the past. Overconfidence can lead to excessive risk-taking and poor decision making, as traders may believe that they have a better understanding of the market than they actually do.

In conclusion, managing risk and understanding the psychological aspects of trading are critical to success in the stock market. By incorporating risk management strategies and recognizing and managing the emotional challenges of trading, traders can increase their chances of success and minimize their potential for losses.

"Successful traders are those who find the balance between discipline and flexibility."

9.2 Money Management Techniques

Money management is a crucial aspect of trading and involves the systematic approach to managing your trading capital. It is the process of determining the appropriate amount of capital to allocate to each trade, as well as determining how much of the trading capital should be kept in reserve. Money management helps traders to limit the potential for significant losses, while also maximizing the chances of long-term success. There are several money management techniques that traders can use to help them manage their capital effectively.

One of the most commonly used money management techniques is the fixed fractional approach, which involves allocating a fixed percentage of your trading capital to each trade. This percentage should be based on your risk tolerance, as well as your overall trading strategy. By allocating a fixed percentage of your capital to each trade, you can limit the potential for significant losses and ensure that you have enough capital to stay in the game over the long-term.

Another money management technique is the position sizing approach, which involves determining the appropriate size of each trade based on the volatility of the underlying asset. This approach involves calculating the amount of capital that should be allocated to each trade based on the average true range (ATR) of the underlying asset. By using the ATR to determine position size, traders can ensure that they are not overexposing themselves to risk in volatile markets.

Another important money management technique is the use of stop losses, which are predetermined levels at which a trader will close a position to limit potential losses. By using stop losses, traders can ensure that they are not taking on too much risk in a single trade, and can help to limit the potential for significant losses.

In conclusion, effective money management is essential to the success of any trader, and it is important to have a systematic approach to managing your trading capital. By using techniques such as the fixed fractional approach, position sizing, and stop losses, traders can help to limit the potential for significant losses and ensure long-term success.

"The secret to successful trading is to find the edge and manage your risk."

9.3 Understanding Psychological Aspects of Trading

Trading is a complex and emotional activity that requires discipline and control. The psychological aspects of trading are just as important as the technical analysis used to make trades. Emotions can play a significant role in the decision-making process and can lead to impulsive decisions that can be detrimental to a trader's success.

Trading psychology can be divided into two main areas: emotions and biases. Emotions, such as fear and greed, can interfere with a trader's judgment and lead to bad decisions. For example, fear of losing money may lead to missed opportunities or premature selling, while greed may cause a trader to hold onto a losing trade too long.

Biases are inherent flaws in thinking that can affect the interpretation of information and the decision-making process. For example, confirmation bias is the tendency to only seek out information that supports a trader's existing beliefs, while neglecting information that contradicts those beliefs. Overconfidence bias can lead a trader to ignore risk and pursue high-risk trades.

To be a successful trader, it is important to understand and manage the psychological aspects of trading. This can be done by developing a trading plan and sticking to it, avoiding impulsive trades, and seeking out impartial information and education. Regular self-reflection and seeking feedback from others can also help traders become more aware of their biases and emotions and how they impact their decision-making.

It is also important to remember that trading success is not a quick process and requires patience, discipline, and a long-term perspective. Trading can be a challenging and humbling experience, but by understanding and managing the psychological aspects of trading, traders can increase their chances of success.

9.4 Avoiding Common Trading Mistakes

One of the biggest factors in the success or failure of a trader is their ability to avoid common trading mistakes. Here are some of the most common mistakes that traders make and tips on how to avoid them:

Over-trading: Over-trading is one of the most common mistakes that traders make. This is when a trader makes too many trades, often in an attempt to make up for previous losses or to chase profits. This can lead to significant losses, as well as increase the risk of burnout. To avoid over-trading, traders should stick to a well-planned trading strategy, and avoid making impulsive trades.

Not having a well-defined trading plan: A well-defined trading plan is a key component of successful trading. Without a plan, traders are more likely to make impulsive decisions, which can lead to losses. To avoid this mistake, traders should take the time to create a detailed trading plan, including the rules for entry and exit, the risk-reward ratio, and the trading style.

Ignoring risk management: Risk management is a critical component of trading success. Traders who ignore risk management are more likely to suffer significant losses, as well as experience increased stress and anxiety. To avoid this mistake, traders should make sure that they have a well-defined risk management plan in place, and that they stick to it.

Failing to diversify: Diversification is a key component of risk management, as it helps to spread risk across multiple assets. Traders who concentrate their investments in a single asset, or in a small group of assets, are more vulnerable to market fluctuations and other risks. To avoid this mistake, traders should make sure to diversify their portfolios, and to invest in a mix of different assets, such as stocks, bonds, and commodities.

Not taking emotions out of trading: Emotions can have a significant impact on trading decisions, and can lead to impulsive and emotional trades. To avoid this mistake, traders should make sure to keep their emotions in check, and to stick to their well-defined trading plan. This may require traders to take breaks when they feel stressed or overwhelmed, and to practice self-care to maintain their emotional well-being.

By avoiding these common mistakes, traders can increase their chances of success and minimize their risk of losses. Additionally, by focusing on risk management, diversification, and emotional well-being, traders can maintain a positive and productive mindset, which is critical for long-term success.

Conclusion and Final Thoughts

Technical analysis is a popular method of predicting market trends and making informed investment decisions. By combining an understanding of chart analysis, technical indicators, support and resistance levels, chart patterns, and trading strategies, traders can develop a comprehensive approach to the markets. However, technical analysis alone is not enough to ensure success in trading. It is important to also consider the psychological aspects of trading and to properly manage risk through sound money management techniques.

The key to success in trading is to have a well-defined plan and to stick to it, regardless of market conditions. This requires discipline and a level of emotional detachment from the markets. Traders must also have a thorough understanding of their own personality and risk tolerance, and be aware of the common trading mistakes that can lead to failure. By taking the time to understand and incorporate these principles into their trading plan, traders can greatly increase their chances of success.

In conclusion, technical analysis is a powerful tool for predicting market trends and making informed investment decisions. However, it is only one aspect of a successful trading strategy. Traders must also consider the psychological and risk management aspects of trading to increase their chances of success. By combining a comprehensive approach with discipline and a well-defined plan, traders can navigate the markets with greater confidence and achieve their financial goals.

Points to Remember

- Risk management is a critical component of successful trading. It involves setting stop-loss orders, managing position sizes, and determining the amount of capital to risk on each trade.
- One of the most common psychological traps that traders fall into is the fear of missing out (FOMO), which can lead to impulsive and irrational trading decisions.
- To avoid emotional trading decisions, traders should have a set of well-defined trading rules and a clear trading plan. It's also important to avoid overtrading and to take breaks from trading when necessary.
- Traders should focus on the process of trading, rather than the outcome of each individual trade. This means evaluating their performance based on their adherence to their trading plan, rather than their P&L.
- Keeping a trading journal can be a helpful way to identify areas for improvement and to track progress over time.
- Traders should also be mindful of their biases, including confirmation bias, overconfidence bias, and recency bias, which can lead to irrational trading decisions.

- Finally, traders should have realistic expectations for their trading performance and should be patient and disciplined in their approach. Successful trading takes time, effort, and continuous learning and improvement.

CHAPTER TEN

Conclusion

Recap of Technical Analysis Basics

Technical analysis is a method used to evaluate securities and make informed investment decisions by analyzing the statistical trends of the financial market. This method is based on the idea that market trends, reflected in the price movements and chart patterns of a security, can be used to predict its future performance.

In this overview of technical analysis, we have covered various aspects of the method, including chart types, trend analysis, technical indicators, support and resistance levels, chart patterns, oscillators, candlestick charting, and trading strategies. We have also discussed the importance of risk management and psychological aspects of trading, and offered advice on avoiding common trading mistakes.

Some of the key technical indicators discussed include moving averages, Bollinger Bands, the Relative Strength Index (RSI), the Stochastic Oscillator, the Moving Average Convergence Divergence (MACD), and momentum indicators like the Moving Average Oscillator, the Relative Strength Oscillator, Williams %R, and the Rate of Change (ROC).

Chart patterns, such as head and shoulders, flag and pennant, triangle, double and triple tops/bottoms, and candlestick patterns like doji, hammer/hanging man, and marubozu, were also covered in detail.

Trading strategies based on technical analysis include trend following, breakout, mean reversion, and moving average crossover strategies. Money management techniques, such as position sizing and stop-loss orders, were discussed as a critical component of successful trading.

In conclusion, technical analysis is a comprehensive method that can be used to make informed investment decisions, but it is important to keep in mind that no single indicator or strategy is foolproof, and that risk management and psychological discipline are essential for success. As with any investment strategy, it is important to continuously educate yourself, remain vigilant, and stay up-to-date on market developments.

Importance of Continuous Learning and Improvement

The financial markets are constantly evolving and it is crucial for traders to continuously improve their skills and knowledge in order to stay ahead of the competition. This requires a commitment to ongoing learning and development. In technical analysis, it is essential to keep up-to-date with the latest trends, new chart patterns, and emerging indicators. In order to achieve success as a trader, it is important to be proactive in seeking out new information, attending workshops and webinars, and participating in online communities dedicated to technical analysis.

It is also important to have a growth mindset and be open to new ideas and perspectives. Technical analysis is a complex discipline that requires time and effort to master, but with continuous learning and improvement, traders can refine their skills and increase their chances of success.

In addition to staying informed, traders must also be willing to experiment and refine their strategies. This can involve testing new indicators, adjusting position sizing, and making changes to trade entry and exit strategies. The goal should always be to continuously improve the chances of success and minimize risk.

In conclusion, continuous learning and improvement are crucial components of successful trading using technical analysis. By staying informed, remaining open to new ideas and perspectives, and being willing to experiment and refine strategies, traders can increase their chances of success and become more effective in their analysis and decision-making.

Final Thoughts on Technical Analysis

Technical analysis is a powerful tool that traders can use to analyze market trends and make informed investment decisions. It has been used successfully for many decades and continues to evolve as new technologies and data become available.

In this book, we have covered the basics of technical analysis, including chart analysis, trends, technical indicators, chart patterns, oscillators, and momentum indicators. We have also explored some of the key advantages and limitations of technical analysis and compared it to fundamental analysis.

It's important to remember that technical analysis is just one aspect of the investment process and should be used in conjunction with other tools and information, such as fundamental analysis and risk management. Traders who use technical analysis should also be aware of the psychological aspects of trading and be disciplined in their approach to avoid making impulsive decisions.

Ultimately, the success of any trading strategy will depend on a trader's ability to analyze the markets accurately and make informed investment decisions. Technical analysis provides a valuable framework for traders to do this, but it is up to each individual trader to develop their own approach and find what works best for them.

In conclusion, technical analysis is a fascinating field that provides traders with a wealth of information and tools to help them navigate the markets and make successful trades. Whether you are a seasoned trader or just starting out, I hope that this book has provided you with a solid foundation in the basics of technical analysis and inspired you to learn more about this exciting field.

The Future of Technical Analysis

Technical analysis is an ever-evolving field, with new technologies and data becoming available all the time. In the coming years, the following developments are likely to shape the future of technical analysis:

Increased use of artificial intelligence (AI) and machine learning: With the growth of big data and the increasing use of AI, traders will likely start to rely more on algorithms and machine learning models to make trading decisions. This is likely to lead to a further evolution of technical analysis, as traders look for new and innovative ways to leverage the vast amounts of data available to them.

Increased use of real-time data: As technology continues to evolve, traders will have access to real-time data at their fingertips. This will allow traders to make more informed decisions and react to market movements much more quickly.

Greater integration with fundamental analysis: Traders are likely to start looking for ways to combine technical analysis with fundamental analysis to get a better understanding of the market. This could lead to the development of new tools and techniques that blend the two approaches.

Greater use of mobile technology: With the growth of mobile technology, traders are likely to start using their smartphones and tablets more often to monitor their portfolios and trade on the go. This will lead to the development of new mobile trading apps and platforms that are optimized for use on smaller screens.

Greater use of blockchain technology: Blockchain technology is likely to become increasingly important in the world of finance, and it could have a significant impact on technical analysis. For example, traders may start to use decentralized exchanges to trade

Cryptocurrencies and other assets, which could change the way traders analyze price trends and make investment decisions.

Overall, the future of technical analysis looks bright, as traders continue to seek new and innovative ways to analyze the markets and make informed investment decisions. The increasing availability of data and technology is likely to drive the evolution of the field and make technical analysis an even more powerful tool for traders in the years to come.

APPENDIX

The appendix section of this book is designed to provide readers with additional resources and information to help them continue their technical analysis journey.

Glossary of Technical Analysis Terms: This section provides definitions of the most common technical analysis terms used in this book, along with explanations of their significance.

Technical Indicators: This section provides a comprehensive list of the most widely used technical indicators, along with definitions and examples of how each one is used in practice.

Resources for Further Study: This section provides a list of online resources, books, and other materials that readers can use to further their understanding of technical analysis and related topics.

Real-World Case Studies: This section provides case studies of real-world investments and trades made using technical analysis. These case studies provide practical examples of how technical analysis can be used in real-world investment situations, and help readers to see how the concepts covered in this book can be applied in practice.

By the end of this appendix, readers should have a complete understanding of the technical analysis process, and be able to use this information to make informed investment decisions. They will also have access to a wealth of resources to help them continue their learning and growth as technical analysts.

Glossary of Technical Analysis Terms

52-Week High/Low: The highest and lowest prices a stock has traded at over the last 52 weeks.

Bollinger Bands: A technical indicator that uses a moving average and standard deviation to plot upper and lower bands around the price chart.

Candlestick Charting: A type of financial chart that uses candlestick patterns to show price action over a given time frame.

Chart Formation: A pattern that forms on a stock or index price chart, indicating a potential change in trend or reversal.

Chart Pattern: A specific pattern that forms on a price chart, such as a head and shoulders, triangle, or flag.

Dow Theory: A technical analysis approach that focuses on trend analysis, market movements, and trends in market averages.

Moving Average: A technical indicator that plots the average price over a set period of time.

Momentum Indicator: A technical indicator that measures the rate of change in price and displays it as a line on a chart.

Oscillator: A technical indicator that oscillates between two extreme values and is used to identify overbought or oversold conditions.

Support and Resistance: Key price levels at which a stock or index is likely to experience buying or selling pressure, respectively.

Technical Indicator: A mathematical calculation based on the price or volume of a security or index, used to help traders make informed investment decisions.

Trend: The general direction of the market, either up, down, or sideways.

Trendline: A line drawn on a chart that connects two or more price points and is used to identify trends and potential reversal points.

Volatility: A measure of the price fluctuations of a security or index, usually calculated using standard deviation.

Final Words

As we come to the end of this book on the basics of technical analysis, it's important to reflect on what we've learned and the significance of these concepts in the world of finance and investment. Technical analysis provides a unique perspective on market trends, enabling traders and investors to make informed decisions based on past price behaviour.

Throughout the chapters, we've explored the fundamentals of technical analysis, including chart analysis, trends, technical indicators, chart patterns, oscillators and momentum indicators, candlestick charting, trading strategies, and risk management. We've also discussed the advantages and limitations of technical analysis, compared it to fundamental analysis, and examined the psychological aspects of trading.

The resources for further study and real-world case studies in the appendix provide opportunities for continued learning and practical application of the concepts covered in this book. Additionally, the glossary of technical analysis terms serves as a helpful reference tool for those who are new to the subject.

We hope that this book has served as a valuable resource for those who are just starting their journey in technical analysis. Whether you're a trader, investor, or simply seeking to gain a deeper understanding of the financial markets, we believe that the knowledge and skills gained from this book will be instrumental in helping you make informed investment decisions.

In closing, we'd like to thank you for taking the time to read this book and we wish you the best of luck on your journey in technical analysis.

9 798889 861348

Printed by Libri Plureos GmbH in Hamburg, Germany